The Great Jimbo James

Written by Phil Cummings
Illustrated by David Cox

An easy-to-read SOLO
for beginning readers

SOLOS

Southwood Books Limited
3 – 5 Islington High Street
London N1 9LQ

First published in Australia by Omnibus Books 1997

Published in the UK under licence from
Omnibus Books by
Southwood Books Limited, 2001.

Reprinted 2001, 2003

Text copyright © Phil Cummings 1997
Illustrations copyright © David Cox 1997

Cover design by Lyn Mitchell

ISBN 1 903207 19 3

Printed in Hong Kong

A CIP catalogue record for this book is available
from the British Library

For Doreen – P.C.

For Toby – D.C.

Chapter 1

Jimbo James had done his shopping. His trolley was so full it was hard to steer.

Jimbo James stopped for a rest.

Lots of people were watching a magician. He was very good. He juggled ... said magic words ...

… pulled scarves from his sleeves and a rabbit from his hat. It looked easy.

Jimbo James smiled. "Hmm," he said. "That looks easy. *I* could be a magician. I *will* be a magician! I will be … *the Great Jimbo James*!"

Chapter 2

At home, Jimbo James found some plastic bottles. "Great," he said. "I can juggle with these." He painted them red, blue, green, yellow and orange.

He found a box. "Aha! This can
be my magic box." He painted the
box black.

Next he found some black cloth.
"This can be my cape," he said.
And he stuck gold stars all over it.

He made a top hat from some
shiny paper, and a wand from a
very thin stick.

Jimbo James looked great, except for his shoes. He put glue on them and sprinkled them with golden glitter. That was much better.

There was only one thing left to do.
He went out and painted his yellow
van black. He put moons, stars and
fireworks all over it. On the sides it
said *The Great Jimbo James.*

Chapter 3

Jimbo James put on his cape, his top hat and his glittering shoes, and went to the library.

The man in the library looked at
him. "I know what you want," he
said. "You want books on magic,
don't you?"

"That's right," said Jimbo James.
"How did you know?"

The man smiled. "Just a lucky guess," he said.

Jimbo James took all the books he could find on magic. In one book there was a picture of a rabbit popping out of a hat.

"Aha!" cried Jimbo James. "I need a *rabbit*."

He went to the pet shop. The lady in the pet shop looked at him.

"I know what you want," she said. "You want a rabbit for a magic show, don't you?"

"That's right," said Jimbo James.
"How did you know?"

The lady smiled. "Just a lucky
guess," she said.

Jimbo James chose a big white rabbit with pink eyes full of magic. "I will call you Rick," he said. "Rick the Magic Rabbit."

The magic rabbit wiggled its ears.

Chapter 4

There was a school near the pet shop. The children called out when they saw Jimbo James. "Are you a magician?" they asked.

"Yes!" cried Jimbo. "I am the Great Jimbo James, and this is Rick the Magic Rabbit."

The children jumped about. "Will you show us your magic?" they asked. *"Please?"*

"Right now?" asked Jimbo.

"Yes, now," said the children.

"In the school hall."

"OK," said Jimbo James.
"Let's go!"

Chapter 5

The school hall had a big stage. Jimbo James put out his plastic bottles, his magic box and his wand.

Last of all he picked up Rick.
"Don't come out till I say the magic
words," he said softly.

Rick wiggled his ears.

Jimbo James put him into the hat.
He was a big rabbit.

"My," said Jimbo James. "You
are almost too fat for the hat, Rick!"

It was time to start the show.

Jimbo James waved his cape, and some of the stars fell off. "Hello!" he cried. "I am the Great Jimbo James!"

"Hooray!" the children shouted.

"First, I will juggle for you."

He picked up his coloured bottles and began to juggle. Red, blue, green, orange, yellow. Up they all went. Up … up … up.

Then *down* they all came!

The yellow one hit him on the head. CLONK!

The orange one hit him on the head. CLONK!

All the other bottles fell on him.
CLONK CLONK CLONK!

The children giggled.

Chapter 6

"For my next trick," said Jimbo James, "I will put these flowers in my magic box. When I open the box, they will be gone."

He waved his magic wand over
the box. "Tah-dah!" he sang.

Jimbo James opened the box.
The flowers were still there!

All the children giggled. They liked this funny magician!

Jimbo James tried another trick. He held up a red scarf. He put it up his sleeve and waved his magic wand. "Tah-dah!" he sang.

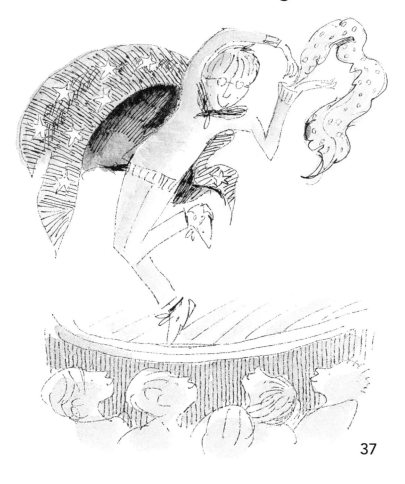

He tried to pull the scarf from his sleeve, but it was gone!

The children pointed to his shoes. "There it is!" they cried.

Jimbo James looked down. The scarf was hanging out of the leg of his trousers. Oh dear! This was not where the scarf should be! He pulled it, and a lot of other coloured scarves came out.

It was very funny to see.

Chapter 7

Jimbo James had one trick left to try.

"For my last trick," he said, "I will pull my magic rabbit, Rick, from the hat."

He waved his magic wand.

The children were quiet. They watched. They waited.

Jimbo James took a deep breath.
He closed his eyes, put his hand into
the hat and … "Tah-dah!" he sang.

He pulled a rabbit out of the hat, but it wasn't Rick. It was a tiny, fluffy baby rabbit!

"Oh!" the children gasped.

Jimbo James put his hand in the hat again. "Tah-dah!" Another little rabbit popped out! "Tah-dah!" Another, and another, and another.

Six little rabbits popped out of the hat! Jimbo James was amazed!

At last he pulled out Rick.
"Hooray!" the children shouted.

Jimbo James looked at all the baby rabbits. Then he looked at Rick. "I will have to change your name," he smiled.

Chapter 8

The next day Jimbo James went shopping. He was going to make a house for the rabbit family. His trolley was so full it was hard to steer.

Jimbo James stopped for a rest. Lots of people were watching an acrobat. He was very good.

Jimbo James smiled. "Hmm," he said. "That looks easy."

Phil Cummings

When I was very young I wanted to be a magician. I wasn't very good at it, but I kept trying. I made a wand, a hat and a cape, and said magic words.

A friend gave me a rabbit, and Mum made a cape for it as well! I tried to make my rabbit disappear, but nothing worked.

One night, while I was asleep, something magic *did* happen. I woke to find that my rabbit had lots of tiny fluffy babies!

David Cox

I have never known anyone exactly like Jimbo James, but I know quite a few people who are something like him and perhaps I am one of them. They are the people who like to try out new things, and they think that if they act out the part, they can do it. The funny thing is that it often works.

When I was asked to illustrate *The Great Jimbo James*, I thought to myself: "I can do that." Just like Jimbo James, see.

More Solos!

Dog Star
Janeen Brian and Ann James

The Best Pet
Penny Matthews and Beth Norling

Fuzz the Famous Fly
Emily Rodda and Tom Jellett

Cat Chocolate
Kate Darling and Mitch Vane

Green Fingers
Emily Rodda and Craig Smith

Gabby's Fair
Robin Klein and Michael Johnson

Watch Out William
Nette Hilton and Beth Norling

The Great Jimbo James
Phil Cummings and David Cox